"Seemingly out of nowhere, Garrett Mostowski has emerged onto the poetry scene, fully formed and displaying impressive range. This maiden collection is a voyage through space, a meditation on youth and old age, a kaleidoscope of biblical and space-age imagery that, in the end, settles into the pattern of a celestial dance. The poems intertwine sorrow with joy and exile with redemption, their gravity livened by humor that emerges like firecrackers lighting up the sky."

—**Connie Buchanan**
Retired freelance book editor

"Garrett Mostowski's poetry makes me feel more alive and hopeful. And courageous. It makes the world seem both enormous and more livable-in. You may consider me biased, as one of the poems is dedicated to me, but I think if you read it, you might see that it's for you too."

—**Gareth Higgins**
Founder, *The Porch*

"Garrett Mostowski's poems are luminous and quickened, whispered secrets caught on the wind, full of pain and wonder, sparked alive by the grace of the mundane. *Lunations* is the kind of book that never leaves you, one you will carry with you all your days."

—**Jimmy Cajoleas**
Author of *Goldeline*

"With *Lunations*, Garrett Mostowski invites the reader on a journey to explore ways of making a new creation amidst our sorrows and losses, ways of making new life amidst climate change and alienation, ways of making connections across previously established divides. *Lunations* presents poetic meditations in conversation with a number of poets and writers, shining light into corners of our individual and shared universes and ultimately reminding us that we are all on this ship together."

—**Shan Overton**
Associate dean of academics, American Baptist College

Lunations

Lunations

Poems

By GARRETT MOSTOWSKI
Foreword by Diane Glancy

RESOURCE *Publications* · Eugene, Oregon

LUNATIONS
Poems

Resource Publications
An Imprint of Wipf and Stock Publishers
199 W. 8th Ave., Suite 3
Eugene, OR 97401

www.wipfandstock.com

PAPERBACK ISBN: 978-1-6667-8487-9
HARDCOVER ISBN: 978-1-6667-8488-6
EBOOK ISBN: 978-1-6667-8489-3

VERSION NUMBER 092523

To Sarah,

What did you expect? The moon?

very alone
in the wildwood
my friend the moon

—Buson

Itinerary

Acknowledgements

To Sarah, Connie, Naima, Kate, Greg, Dad, Mom, Tim Moran and the whole Fort Street family, Kerouac's in Columbus, Matt Casey, Anders, Joey, Josh, Trinity Episcopal Church, Andy, Karen, Porsha, Rachel, Lucinda, Molly, Taylor, Andrew, Donna, Walter, Ruth, Gareth, Shan, Denise, Drew, Diane Glancy, Ross Gay, the whole creative writing and public theology cohort at Pittsburgh Theological Seminary, Megan, Abigail, Shari, Dayle, the whole Continuing Education Department at Princeton Theological for helping me dream, and to Sarah James and the whole team at Clerestory for use of and originally publishing "The Truth" and "Judgment".

And to anyone I may have forgotten.

Thank you all for believing in me when I didn't believe in myself, for encouraging me, for remaining in my orbit.

Foreword

It is the moon that is paradigm for Mostowski's work. The moon—which is the work of thy hands, which thou hast ordained—Psalm 8:3. The gray/white agate in the sky. But this is no ordinary marble game.

Lunations is about shape. The shape of language. The shape of the past. The shape of memory. The shape of the white object that appears most nights in the sky with the thrust of its rise and fall.

For the precious things put forth by the moon—Deuteronomy 6:14. But what effect does the moon have on anything growing in a meadow? Unless crops are the dreams in the field of sleep—harvesting thought-patterns that have to be sorted out—saying, this is what it is for Mostowski—what survives the waning and waxing. It is the search for voice to say how it was and how it all happened. Lunations is a ceremony—a tale of how identity came to be. A centering on relationships. On the movement of the repetition of phases returning with their differences.

To look at the moon is to see a battered shape in the dark sky. Hit by meteors and whatever space-matter flies by and doesn't miss. The pock-marked moon. The battered moon. The ragged moon. The chalk-dust moon. The perfect image for the structure of family. The shape of the book in general—and the shape of the poems themselves as varied as the phases of the moon. Even the tornadic shape of faith.

In this collection, it is an anaphoric moon with its repetitions. New moon or crescent moon / quarter moon / gibbous moon between quarter and full / then the full moon—and back—all over again. These poems move with the same turning. A heavy moon that carries baggage. But Mostowski gives the moon a lift when it seems to be sagging in the sky with the crane of his language. It is the welcome message from the captain's journal.

Diane Glancy, author of *Psalm to Whom(e)*

new moons

you always expect them to be there

somewhere in the middle of the night

sky but every now and then

they've disappeared

you're worried they'll come home again   dressy hair

messed   glasses down their nose at a tilt

buttons from the shirt you gave them

missing   threads frayed pulled

loose and you know you just have to say

to yourself that they only leave you

periodically and you know what they said

about their consistency it's not abandonment

if they've shown up recently

but they don't know the darkness still

won't conceal the holes dotting their face

and besides they can't help it anyway the sneaking

around to hide in the light

of our dying

star

haibun for the earth

If I said this wasn't goodbye, only see you soon, I'd be lying. Hoping, too. I'd be avoiding the inevitable that already came to conclude: That whoever you are and whatever this is it's distant | removed. There's no recourse in any court of any land, no power in heaven that could bring me to you, or you to me--except we. Us I mean. One day, we could determine what we want this to be. And live according to it. We are free to meet wherever

we choose & till then
I'll keep scribbling ways I've missed
all your greens & blues

the politicians

They have made the decision
to let the world decide
who will live
and who must finally lie.

Let the climate naturally
select--or the god if you'd
prefer--which people it actually
chooses.

They turned the world into a game
where everyone clings
tight--tries to never change--
has never ever been wrong.

This is worse than declaring war on someone's home
it's children losing parents, waiting for rescue
dying alone.

advent horizon

for Ursula Leguin

surrounding these words

there's light   so dark it swallows

silence eats moons stars

captain's journal: blast off

alone
up there
build a city there
alone build a city
up there alone build a city up there alone build a city up there
alone
build a city
alone build a city up there alone build a city up there alone build
a city
up there alone
build a city up
there alone
build

overheard onboard #1

for/after Mary Oliver

if the only question is

how to love a pale blue dot

someone should admit

some of us simply

can't

waxing crescent

we rarely catch up

to this cusp

where shadows hide

our crater-shaped hearts

kaboom

kaboom

here we are

two fallen stars

atop hemp wicks

glued in saucy

wax

flailing

in the draft

of our room

the science behind our experiments

There are always many things said in any case of he-said-she-said, or (in this instance) he-said-he-said: some theologian and astronomer--the tragicomedy between them.

Really, all the astronomer told the theologian was that the earth was not flat, the sun had never moved, and the moon had its own reasons for rising how, when it did, 'like a good man [sic]: principled.'

Then he put his hands up and said he wished the theologian wouldn't stay so stuck in the universe unwilling or unable to move even one contemporary unit of measurement in any of the infinite common directions.

It was one of those rain-soaked days in history we all read about in text books, a day when enough became exactly what it is, and, as we know, when enough becomes exactly what it is, everything's extra-extra read all about it.

Which is why when the theologian didn't respond to the astronomer immediately, but instead started scouring his copies of sacred texts with overcast eyes--

ripping out pictures of planets and suns--and sighed, opened his mouth to say nothing, the astronomer understood completely.

Finally, the theologian cleared his throat of dust and the other particles orchestrating his being in time and said to the astronomer from on high,

"Well, perhaps the moon rises
for the hell of it."

Then, he sentenced him to death.

overheard onboard #2

my mother says

she loves me

my father says

i have gifts

but i've never

believed them

before this

meteor showers

She enjoys them most evenings.
But not tonight.
Blugh.

She says it's like running
on earth, some days her legs are roots, not jelly;

sometimes she loves the
putting-one-foot-in-front-of-the-other-ness
of it all, she says;

and she almost misses each forgotten step
that carried her across a continent,

that feeling she gets when
she sort of stops
inside

her body as she continues jogging on
and on

until she becomes fully
present to her
power,

until she is a force not just something
exerting it.

until she's human being,
she says, not just human
doing.

And, there are other days she doesn't care
for any of it -

the luke-warm rush over her
naked frame, the suds from the special soap
she uses to smile,

the chill of the world
after the curtain's pulled back,

the walk over eggshells
into her room to sleep next to
someone she's trying to learn to love

temporarily--all this, all these things
to her, sometimes,

they soul-suck the tedium of space
nights, turning devotion
to chore.

And so, tonight,
she didn't enjoy it.

captain's journal: how not to be afraid

for Gareth Higgins

You don't know what I'm gonna say,
And I don't know what you're gonna think.
So, let's begin with this: Do not be afraid.

A chair collides with a TV but only part of me breaks.
My father never learned how to set down his drinks.
And, I never figured out how to teach him, what I could say.

He huffed, stamped--paced.
Snatched wet glass after wet glass from the sink.
Let's come back to this now: Do not be afraid.

After the glasses shattered, a bloody palm slapped my face.
Cheeks rippled into streams, heated up, flushed pink.
How much more would you like me to say?

My chin is lifted, eyes touching his, when he says,
"you won't amount to a god damn thing."
Now, repeat after me: Do not be afraid.

moons half full

we should note: while they lay most things bare

in their luster, gazing into billions of inverted

domes depressed by the explosions

of whatever they might call world

history, from a distance it seems

the sulfur-fires of their past settled

the armageddons and left crumbed

ejecta scattered across their floors & walls

and what they thought spelled their world's end

turned out to be piles of stones/stacks of broken sticks

moon stones

they've been rolled ground
to powder

and now they are the nothing
left: naked bodies baked

or dust-bones un-mooned
taken to market   sold by you

+

is there anything like them
that doesn't get tired

of waiting and
waiting

things healed by being
left alone   crumbled

+

they're broken like
you are

and if you listen
they cry, too

captain's journal: cupid revised

for & after Rhinna D. Espaillat

I couldn't see what my drunk mother saw so clear:
I didn't suffer from love, but self-enchantment.
"Where's the problem-child with no capacity to pay attention,"
she said & stumbled into my room, tossing loaves at bedside beers.

My windows were closed as cool evening breezes
blew by. She crossed to them, sneered, "First boy to die from a s--"
I watched her lift the clasp, draw in the panes as
wind dropped through my curtains from the eaves.

"She could send you," my mother said, forgetting again,
"tile the plains of every land, the side of every hill."
she could say she cannot love you till
you've sorted salt from the ocean.

That's when I cupped a hand over my ear,
as if to listen. "I said," she shouted, "I'll be damned--"
I blasted past, handed her broken, magic bands and
looked back as her smiling lips drooled out tears.

space walk(s)

this is the fall:

                    the long awakening

from a womb

                    & dreaming innocence

to that first step

                    out of the garden

into existence

                    from who am I

into what will happen

                    to us all

shiver-shivers

                    grunts & groans

tummies rumbling

                    an 'I' rising to speak

        moan

captain's journal: the astronomers

They have to learn how to write again.
It's painful   humbling--

their hands and wrists fused together like
new lovers spooning in a twin.

+

Research today was slow. And they
stared off. Stopped. Kept going

report-by-report, commanding the fog
"Part, part." Until voila! it lifted away.

overheard onboard #3

we will remember when
we used to drive our cars the

way our arms rolled
down windows

how we always looked back
before leaving

home to see
what might be coming

captain's journal: riding bikes

I remember dirt jammed into the hollow parts of our handle bars.
The frayed grass and swishy jackets flapping in the wind around
my hands. Riding side-saddle only to ghostie our rides into fallow
fields we didn't know were eroding.

I remember, at the end of the day, my mother, the badger,
reminding me, "Bring it inside and lock the gate!"

+

I learned what it meant to pull away
from chain-linked fences that threatened to wrest my grips and
strip
my brakes, as the Backyard Boys popped wheelies to start
their morning with a race to the wild trees.

+

There are not enough fingers and toes in my family to count the
nights my father wiped away the mistakes I left all over the spokes,
rims, and frame.

+

He often wondered if I had been raised in a barn--what, with the
way the garage door gaped as I peeled out of our cinder drive.

+

His stood stock still and upright, glinting in the dark corner of our garage, where it stands still today. He said it would always be there for me, waiting for days filled with flat-tires, afternoons of dislocated chains, when my habit of not-using-the-kickstand-parking culminated in cables stripped and frayed worse than the rubber grips he swore he just replaced.

+

If he could, he would ask me if I used my kickstand today. And I would laugh and say maybe, if I remembered to remember. If I could, I would tell him, "My habits changed when you weren't around to fix everything."

waxing gibbous

after Ross Gay

by which we mean all this protuberant talk

by which we mean whatever bulges eyes to white

we mean this swelling   like my inflamed and distended

bowels that distort the otherwise flat surface of my stomach

by which I mean I'm bloated and excessive in size and I know

it's from the pressure I feel on the inside to thrust myself into the

receding outlines of your spheres that slid between the folds

that creased the vaults beneath our sheets where our toes

intertwine till tingled   by which I mean they form the

only interior angles 'round   as we lie beneath

flat one-hundred-eighty degrees

approaching climax

overheard onboard #4

Are pen caps necessary?

Or do we just like the aesthetic?

Have a hard time

separating?

guide to the space music library

for Enzo & Ocean Vuong

I like to begin any work session with "Hopefull"--
the song, not the entire EP--
all the ascending and
whatnot puts me in a mood.

Next, I'll add "Raindrops" on Far & Away.
The almost urgent melancholy it stirs within me
is like snatching a cup to empty a case
of beer and most nights I need that.

Then: "Longing for Lilly."
Because, who isn't?
And how is she?

"Red Dawn" is sometimes good
for the quietly dramatic moments
of your WIP, stepping tones &
sprinkling pings intertwined--
up, down, up, down, splash--
like a fairy flicking their wand.

It always helps me dramatize
whatever I've divined.

For voice-driven work, the high notes of "Abandoned"

will leave you feeling both lost
and found and somehow more
hopeful than "Hopefull," which is why I recommend keeping it off
the main playlist,
and instead putting it to the side, as a single, for endlessly looping
encores after another god damn form rejection
that's convinced you it might be time to die.

"Misty Wind" feels like hide-and-seek
outside with all the neighbor kids at night.
Boundaries stretched across 3,4,5 backyards
plus Papaw's creepy woods across the street. Or,
better, it's like sneaking off to abandoned automotive factories
under dull orange lights that somehow look purple when you stare
at them.
No: it feels like walking in the snow at night under a half moon and
looking up at some hollow cathedral.

I can't recommend it in good faith,
but I know a lot of people (read: 2) that
have had a lot of success with "Mystic River."
For me, it feels too much like grinding in the eighth
Final Fantasy on some super slow Tuesday afternoon
while it rains. And, I don't love that. But give it a try, you might.

If you are beginning that next epic fantasy,
make sure you keep "Castaway" in your rotation.
It will come in handy when your hero sets off on their journey.
Takes me back to canoeing the Anduin under
the canopy of Lothlorien during the Fall of
Amroth yesterday evening.

Try to always end with "Silver Sky" and
make sure you've stopped working,
make sure you close your eyes,
make sure you're breathing,

imagine all the things
you're grateful for being.

space-time continuum: chronos

it's an operator saying, One minute please.
and after that, Another minute okay.
One moment, Pardon, one more,
would you hold for me until
Hello? Wait to connect

+

it's an assembly line conveying every thin second
hand meant for watches & clocks to fill us with the hope
we will be able to construct minutes, hours, and days
well-spent

+

it's what we used to endure--people rushing through airports
where we made our home, looking neither left nor correct,
and forgetting both what's ahead and behind of them, as they
pull the slots of their inbox, refreshing for news
of another job they hope to land soon

+

it's a room with sign-in sheets & secretaries.
rainy spring days when teachers show students
how to count by looking at a calendar and measuring
how far the beginning separated from what comes next

flutter moon

you

make me flutter

moon   give me stars

for what'll only be remembered

as surviving amidst what we do not yet know

are our last hours

adrift

captain's journal: hymn to the moon

for/after Lady Mary Wortley Montagu

silvered god of secrets
shared at night,

direct my walk through
this decompression chamber.

your unconscious witness
of my concealed delights--

the lovers, the muses, the mass
of their frames

against mine--is the same
pale beam that lights

where I used
to rove.

apologize for me
to the abandoned

those practicing
serenities amidst

the burning
grove.

full moon

we said we played
so much tennis green wires
littered the sand on that beach.
and after, I put my coffee cup
lips to both of your knees,
thighs, hips, the cherry
you picked.

rockets blasted off and holy
water splashed against the throne
of our thighs, rubber band tongues
flicked, smacked our teeth as they played
gravel roads grinding cement.
swells ripped, blew--smashed. bleat
& blather. whimper. whimper. whine.

there, caught up in the ink
poured over the world, we smelled fish
flown in from Spain, and all the flowers you said
needed shelter from rain. waves rolled over tossed
& turned, sea foam dripped down our legs.
in the distance, wind turbines reeled,
beacons blinking, blinking, blinking--red.

and when, eventually, we dreamed,
deserts blossomed, seas dried, too.

And you heard babies laughing
and we became parents
saying--oo! Then, some fire
caught the world's end,
ashen skies turned blue.

supermoon

for/after Gerard Manley Hopkins

I awoke midsummer
drunk-dialed my wife
in the soft white and
walk of what felt early.

The sun, it seemed, was coming
up--like a finger-nail--a candle
maybe, or fruit, too, and waning,
listless even--no brighter than the

edge of a pale stool hid behind
a counter. Or was it the front
half of the barrow's wheel,
one snowy peak. Then

its cratered cusp. Gasp--what
a fluke. This was the other light, the one
pulling cloud after cloud, over my wooly eyes,
saying this is a good time for falling back asleep.

moon and me

for/after Carl Sandburg

                    tea leaves
                    were picked
                  to sell the west
                to the highest bidder
             not sand dealers drilling canals
                  double-time
             resisting a planet due to revise
                    its future
forecasts   then the moon said   bye-bye, baby,
     I'll see you in a few years--promise   and
       the sky's empty   everything's empty
              moon and me don't talk   we
             only listen to the TV yell at each
                other when the dog barks

space-time continuum: kairos

for/after Scott Cairns

you can spell it aha
use any sound made
when you learn something lost
has been

+

you can't pay clocks
to confess its truth:
a lifetime can be lived
on a boring afternoon

+

it's a friend saying, on days like this
I forget winter exists, or I went all week
not knowing what month it had been,
or I was parked on the Thursday side
Wednesday

+

it's listening to a playlist as large
as the universe next to _____and feeling like you
were there, too, before the beginning, where there
was no sound, and we were one thing holding
each other in the milk of the stars

meteor fields

for/after R.S. Thomas

have you ever wondered who is awake at this hour
among the world's acres of grass

devouring epitaphs on stones,
where we are a shadow, where a shadow stains

the withered ground, where the ground narrates
past and future, where the future is vague in truth

due to the nature of shadows ordained
to encroach upon an immaterial tide,

the same tide swallowing the lichen, brick, lights,
and faces, stone faces, with names we knew and named

and who no longer lie awake beneath the place
where dozens of flowers rot in a mound

left to decompose, where, one day, we'll die,
where dying is a moment in time retained by soil

forever, where forever is the dream of rain, unending
rain in the desert, where deserts are truer than anything

except the god, who is silent as our bones
floating through space.

overheard onboard #5

It didn't fit. Nothing seemed to.

He tried it this way. that.

Even upside-down.

She watched each grunting attempt, and then asked,

"Are you sure it's not right?"

"I tried it," he said.

"I wonder if you should try again?"

Cram. Stuff. Jam. Slide--

Slip.

"That's it."

waning gibbous

we drove together in a red rental
until the world ended
at some rock
beach

waves alone applauded
as we curled
beneath outcropped
boulders, terrestrial dad bods

you said something

about the trains how they were

still

under orange lights

decommissioned or obsolete

I don't know
but in the morning
I was, too,
and found a blue car

and drove away

from the sea and   from you

and   all the way back to

anonymity

the truth

The velvet sky is deep-blue water:
so full of itself it's been
emptied,

relegated to some brooding mystery--
or maybe, an outward sign of
what we've felt was true all along:

nobody was ever alone,
they've just been left
wondering.

You and I don't live on bread alone,
But this is the loaf we need to eat--
the cup we've dropped and didn't drink--the

broken strings of
yet-to-be-kept promises
vaulted in gathered memories--

like little lights thrown into shadowed skies, or
the last speck of night sinking to the bottom of all that's blue,
where a voice cries out:

Remember,
this is the way
to feel the truth.

captain's journal: mental health day

for/after James Weldon Johnson

Sometimes the blue skies block me,
and puffy white clouds can feel clingy;
So, I've thought up a way to transform cheer
      into gloom.

If the path continues to glow, brightened by fortune,
gold, and privilege, a glad defiance will rattle my bones,
till I pierce the sky with a croak.
      And wallow.
      Wallow.

I've all but erased my perfect childhood, and soon,
I'll trash whatever grace I've received;
No days are great, no time is fun, and in my arms
I cradle two swans
      writhing,
      broken-necked,

      singing.

overheard onboard #6

the cyberwars are coming

because we are too afraid

of death to kill ourselves

with nuclearity & its

accompanying accoutrements

moon half empty

I am counting on the wells mortared far below
to keep my final breaths safe for me,
those draining out of this room
and into space.

I will make waves
until the waves make waves,
until the news of my melancholies
reach the staffs working for the agency.

Some told me
risk. Some accept.
Others forgive. But, I would
rather drown draped in my very own dress.

I am water already--lifted & churned--
filling up all that's been emptied
by the hollow wind
we're breathing out.

I have been before (and will become again)
nothing--a twitch, a burst, just some
deep breath who once thought
it was thinking.

captain's journal: space haikus

blooming flowers burst
in her hair & autumn winds
brush over her ears

+

she said follow me
to church & so we raced
until I was lost

+

if my brain was a
world its moon would not find
stars to reveal night

+

fall's divorce rippled
evaporating onshore
into April's clouds

+

i shaded my soul
Cerulean the day we
lost Dandelion

+

they say spring babies
are far too young to recall
September's divorce

+

on hands/knees praying
under wildfire suns
dry throats cough & wheeze

+

she's on the other
side of rivers between us
a witch's cauldron

overheard onboard #7

there isn't much left

to do

we need someone yet

to exist

captain's journal: friday night

this is Friday night

in space

after my work is done

after sunset after nine after

earth's households have spilled

into restaurant booths and out or

stayed behind to have one

or a few more

this is Friday night behind a bottle

of 30 year old Malbec the agency assured me

even a novice somm should like

waning crescent

if you're reading
this it's

fate welcome to the club of
we don't know what

to do

or say

captain's journal: scribbles

I'm weary
day was
long sorry
I have well
new moon
was due
at midnight
plus I
had obligations
like the uh
video reading
for my most
recent
alma
mater
today
after work
that I
had to read
at and
oh just
come over
already
I'm so
lonely this
winter

eventide
let's see what's
possible
on platform
beds &
can you like
this if
you chose
to read
this far
instead of
moving on
to whoever
whatever
else
might've grabbed
your attention
in the middle
of this
in-person
silence

and sorry

I'm sorry
I didn't
look I
just didn't
know I was-
n't allowed
to drink
and look
if your're
already
with someone
else it's

fine just
tell me what
y'all'll be
up to later
because
I might
get up to
it too
as I float
back and
also
farther away
into some
collection
of
essays

pale weariness

for/after Percy Bysshe Shelley

pale weariness   climbing heaven

gazing earth   companionless

among planets and stars

wandering like an eye

that finds no worth

in consistency

overheard onboard #8

it's not that

you weren't worth

fighting for

it's that

you were worth

not-fighting for

sestina for a moonless day

for Diane Glancy

I'm happy to tender
a shrug of resignation, mostly out of paranoia
brain fog
and a raven
nested inside the fresh fleece
I wanted to wear over this morning's tea.

This is over-steeped. The tea,
I mean, and it's tender,
too; easy to slice through like my fleece.
Pardon the irregularity: it's the paranoia
flaring up again. And besides, I can quote the raven
too, "[Insert grave sounds and ellipsis] Beware collisions with fog!"

Fog,
it turns out, is the world brewed to tea
plus the astringency of lemon mated with lime--something the
raven
can drink--acrid, tender.
And, here comes the paranoia:
Who took my fleece?

I'm sure you know how fleece
and fog
drape their idiosyncratic statements over paranoia

like my mouth sipping at your lips trying to extract a drop of tea;
or, like our space ship turned tender
in a rush of solar wind that startles even the raven.

I have accepted her, the raven:
stuffed with fleece,
wings tender
with fog
and her love of tea,
her paranoia.

Here's what I really mean: paranoia
is when the raven
starts playing penguin in a nice hot-potta papaw's tea.
Gets soaked through to its fleece
beneath its sweater of fog
and the glue holding it together goes tender

in the heat. What she wants is paranoia--my god damn fleece
taken from me. It was the raven, too. But, never mind. This is all
a fog--
these tender, cold cups of tea.

the edge

i've been to it

seen

that it

looks like

it might

be better

to end this

already

dark moon

we don't feel anything
when you come around
only secondhand sensations
of hope for belonging
an appetite to hear
you say what we
will not:

god damn us for leaving
our mother.

but it's just an expression.
it doesn't mean anything.

it's lips and teeth
weaving what
we've emptied
again at your feet,
so you might see we've had
all the thoughts you prayed
we wouldn't think.

captain's journal: our first time

i remember your body

itching after rolling

naked in the alfalfa

and lying awake till

high noon

hands enmeshed

with brown roots hidden

in the blonde

of the sky

metaverse

for/after Emily Dickinson

moon was born

a night or two ago
and now she turns

from the metaverse below

her forehead Barbie blonde
cheeks an agate scooped

from a once-craggy pond
filled with leftover dews

she's who's most like me
in a world of gemstone lips

where what you think must be
us smiling really isn't it's trinkets--

hats, curtains, shoes--the weight of a life
spent as dust   chasing the afterlight

captain's journal: final transmission

for/after Tracey K. Smith

I am pocked and white

like this morning's newspaper

after the rain,

like the animals

who made me.

+

I'm floating

far

away from you,

but

parallel, too.

+

we are only

six light minutes away

but it might as well be

something more impossible than that.

Abyssi, maybe.

And still, we are orbiting

around the same center.

+

And while you zap

and zip away into a new kind of life,

flittering and fluttering between identities

around our Sol, I will be crawling along

beside you, at my own pace,

watching with one blinking eye

all the smoke of the world turn blue.

+

I am with you

in spirit

if you see what I mean--

connected. At peace.

And that is enough for me.

But I don't know how much it is for you.

+

I don't have a lot of time to buzz in circles;

I only have a few seconds to sneak

Through this straight stretch

of an ever-widening

cosmic circus

ring.

+

Here's why I'm slow:

I wear a wrist compass; and

I am only sometimes an orange slice

at night; and far behind you, technologically;

not always able to respond right away;

and have only just begun my living;

It is because I am away,

but still here with you,

just observing

everything

in my

time

with space.

armageddon

this is the mechanism used

to universally contain us:

the remembrance of

trauma mixed with

our compound

-ed histories

heavy & un-

able to go

with us

into sp-

ace

judgement

It is not always a guilt-and-punishment salve to put over what's
been hurting.
It's also a moment--
a never-ending sentence jotted down as some significant event
inside of time as 'history' for whoever may still be reading this
soon; it's an
enjambed tomb becoming something even as it refuses to keep
anything else alive,
save for its own recycled memory.
But, what's crazy is this: It wrapped the future into some present
for all those involved
and to a lesser degree those not involved at all beyond being gath-
ered with others like them.
And, this is all because 'It has been written,' you know.
It is sometimes these guilts
and often times these punishments,
but it's never-ever this: Who wrote these sentences?
Who's stating these things? And, find out this: Why?
And, who the hell's in charge of making history?
And, what should we be saying now
to have our progeny be where we hoped we'd be by now
but aren't? It's all this, too: Pending boughs, hovering in the wind;
Waiting to see where we will all eventually go;
Wondering what the god is thinking;
Wishing we could judge a tree by where it had grown;
And praying for our own particular endings.

captain's journal: leaving orbit

I'm told we'll be sailing soon.

We have somewhere to go.

And, really, I need to get going.

But, who knows where to?

The crew are in no rush because they know we'll soon
be gliding over the crests of waves we could only
imagine before, dipping down into some sea
tucked into a valley from our seat up here
but what's really two continents on
either side of a sea we pray still teems.

All this will sound like someone called
to me--out loud--saying,
"Are the cosmos only an algorithm?
Or would you like for us to meet?"

And now, I'm staring down into the hidden darkness of the rift
opening beneath our hull, dropping the ship that will
take us to go wherever we've been going,
and I just can't help but think,
"What's going on? And,
who's doing this?"

And, I can't forget that the sun will never rise here.
But I think I will always expect it to set. And maybe
that's a good thing. This isn't the beginning
of draughts drawn from empty, embittered seas.
It doesn't paint the end of all blue skies,

stars...

It's a beginning

not an end

to everything.

overheard onboard #9

those who've arrived didn't

necessarily intend

to arrive

they only intended to resist

whatever kept them

from a different

kind of

breath

utopia

It is as real as a state of mind, existing
and not existing at the same time; it's
as palpable as last night's dream

this morning.

It's what you understand you want to do
as you realize what you have done
isn't what you want to do at all,

it's what you hate.

It's literally without place--yes--
But it's not without spirit. It isn't lacking little rootlets--
Look! nouns and verbs submerged in what amounts

to conscience.

It's what grants feet the grounds for chasing after wind,
hurls blueprints against the screen behind our closed eyes
and leads us from 'in the beginning' all the way to

an end.